HIGHER EDUCATION IN INDIA

HIGHER EDUCATION IN INDIA

ITS POSITION AND CLAIMS

SIR RAYMOND WEST

GYAN

Published by

Gyan Publishing House
5, Ansari Road
Daryaganj, New Delhi-110002
Phone: 011-47034999, 9811692060
E-mail: books@gyanbooks.com

Distribution Network
gyanbooks.com
India, USA, Canada, UK, Australia

ISBN: 978-93-7097-803-4 (HB)

First Published, 1892

2nd Impression 2025

Printed at: Gyan Press, Delhi.

HIGHER EDUCATION IN INDIA: ITS POSITION AND CLAIMS
Arthur SIR RAYMOND WEST

HIGHER EDUCATION IN INDIA:

ITS POSITION AND CLAIMS.

BY

SIR RAYMOND WEST.

PRESIDENT OF THE INDIAN SECTION.

HIGHER EDUCATION IN INDIA:

ITS POSITION AND CLAIMS.

LADIES AND GENTLEMEN,—

I feel very deeply the honour you have done me in electing me President of the Indian Section of this Congress of Oriental Scholars. In thanking you for the distinction you have conferred upon me, I could have wished to mark my appreciation of it, and, if possible, justify your choice, by some definite and original contribution to your proceedings, as the result of research in some hitherto unworked field. But the notice I received was very brief, and my books and papers, recently arrived from India, are not yet so arranged as to be readily available for reference and citation. Under these circumstances I have resolved to take as the subject of my address to you a topic with which my daily life, as an official in India, has made me more or less familiar. In offering some observations on the position of the Higher Education in India I shall dwell on a topic which, though not of a recondite nature, is yet of great importance, and must have a special interest for scholars like yourselves, zealous for the cultivation of solid and fruitful learning amongst a people upon whose history and literature your attention has been fixed through many studious years. India holds a place, and a not inconsiderable one, in the history of human thought. It may have much still to contribute to the ideas and the impulses, to the longings, hopes, and sympathies, which are the moving forces of mankind. That its intellectual wealth should be developed and directed aright is a matter that concerns all men, but especially the subjects of Her Majesty the Queen-Empress who are immediately responsible for the welfare and honour of this great dependency. These considerations may, perhaps, be held to excuse me for endeavouring to bring about something like a general consensus of opinion in appreciating what has been accomplished already, in recognising defects in the existing system of education, and in indicating the means by which a further great and continuous progress may be ensured.

Seeing the extent of my subject in its modern and practical aspect, I cannot at present dwell at any length on the ancient learning of the Hindus, on the means by which it was nurtured and propagated, on the schools of philosophy, the seminaries of Vedantic study, the rivalries of the orthodox and the ascetics, or the patronage of scholars by the princes and chiefs, who thus hoped both to gain a divine guidance in their undertakings, and to win an eternal commemoration of their great deeds. Our attention will no doubt be drawn to these subjects in some of the learned papers that will be read before us. I propose only to glance at one or two points as a necessary introduction to the remarks which are to follow.

A distribution of functions and division of labour have from the earliest times been recognised in the Brahminical system as part of the ordination of Providence. The Brahmins gave a sacred import to what was merely a convenient arrangement, an absolute unqualified value to virtues and capacities of conditional and limited utility. What we call principles are generally rules or propositions which, though just and true as applied to facts within a certain range, become erroneous when extended to a wider application. The subtilty of things exceeds the subtilty of words, and the phrase or formula which was highly valuable as a summation or a symbol of actual observation or experience, becomes misleading when it is assigned an independent value and made to control facts instead of representing them. Thus, as particular qualities and capacities are closely connected with particular avocations, the Brahmins conceived virtues and mental perfections as the specific characteristics of castes rather than as the attributes of developed and cultivated humanity. The common background of identical mutual needs, of duties and rights, subject only to modal variations, was too much overlooked, just as in Europe until recent times the dominance of one or another set of human perfections was exclusively accepted by one or another class as all-important. In India no man, it was thought, could be expected to fill out the whole sphere of moral and intellectual greatness; in Europe that sphere itself was contracted according to the needs or narrow experience of this or that class; and virtue for all mankind was, according to different theories, to be based on different ideals. This involved a clashing and contradiction which the Brahmin avoided by his distribution of moral obligations, but it led by degrees to higher and higher conceptions of what was possible and desirable for the progress and perfection of the human race on a footing of substantial moral equality. It allowed for that final adjustment of each individual to his proper place in the thinking and acting world by which the greatest economy of moral and material forces was to be secured, while caste and its consequences bound men down by ever-multiplied restrictions to narrowness, stagnation, and timidity in thought and action.

The higher education of Ancient India was, in substance, the education of the Brahminical class conceived as the sole and sacred depositaries of enlarged thought and elevated morality. The attempt, nay, the mere desire, to scale the heights of learning was deemed a grievous offence in one belonging to an inferior caste. The Brahmins, by renouncing all ideas of military prowess and dominion, as inconsistent with the proper attributes of their caste, extinguished the jealousy of the Kshatriya princes who then, on account both of the mental superiority and of the sacred character of the unwarlike "lords of the earth," became their generous patrons and pupils. The Brahmins were comparatively insensible to the stimulus of power, honours, and fortune, which in these days operate not less strongly on them than on others; but the love of learning, and of intellectual activity for their own sakes, ruled amongst them, with not less force than afterwards prevailed amongst some of the monastic orders of Europe. Their experience in the conduct of human affairs being very limited, and the pictures of Governments they looked on being rather those of individual caprices than of the conflicts of political ideas, and the movement of masses or parties with desires and aims wrought by mutual reaction to this or that resultant force, they could not and did not write history. From their placid standpoint of immeasurable religious superiority they looked on with real or affected indifference. But in the other chief spheres of mental activity, such as mathematics, philosophy, and poetry, they made a progress in many cases exceeding that of their

European contemporaries. The contact of mind with mind, the minute familiarity with the most captivating thoughts of the past, acquired by long years of rote learning and verbal analysis, kept the intellectual life in existence, vigorous within its limits, if not progressive, as under the rule of the schoolmen and of Avenoes's Aristotelism was afterwards the case in Europe. But the capacity for expansion and growth had evidently been lost even before the irruption of the Mahomedans. The far-ranging conquests and conversions of Islam in India narrowed the field for the chance growth of individual genius; but the culminating point of Brahminical learning had already been reached, and it seems highly improbable that any Galileo or Bacon would have arisen to break down old ideas and force the acceptance of a new world of light on recipients triply enveloped in learned misconceptions and prejudices, without rivals or enemies, and regarding as abominable anything which should touch their cherished traditions and beliefs.

Amid the sea of Mahomedan conquest there were always some islands of Hindu independence. In the territories of the Rajput princes, and in the chiefships which arose on the decay of the Mogul dynasties, Brahminical learning circled round and round in a barren sphere of commentary exigesis and verbal controversy. Learning was kept alive, and the valuable treasures of the past were in part preserved, but with no fresh gifts to human thought of appreciable value. For centuries the case of India was as the case of Greece during its long domination by the Romans. The capacity to acquire, to imitate, to work on ground already prepared, existed; the capacity to create and produce, to estimate with penetrating judgment and a just sense of proportion, had fallen into a state of trance or torpor amid its vaporous environment of unsubstantial learning. Yet the hereditary intellectual faculty had not perished. It only awaited contact with a living, vigorous, growing organism, to itself awaken again into new activity. The right point of view from which to look out on the problems of human nature and life had been lost. The slavish submission to authority, and to the dead-letter of the sacred writings, deepened from age to age. It required a mighty shock to break these bonds asunder. This shock was given by the British conquests, and by the energy with which European ideas in every sphere were forced on the attention of Hindu scholars and thinkers in the last century. Had the new light been as gladly welcomed as that which spread over Europe at the revival of learning, we might ere now have witnessed a complete renascence of the native intellect. The variety of life, the infinite conflict of contending interests, which in Europe remoulded the boons of antiquity to the uses of modern society, were in a great measure wanting in India. The severance of learning and speculative power from the pursuits and the endless suggestiveness of practical life was almost complete. Religion everywhere stood forth with menacing mien to guard the traditional learning and philosophy from intrusion, examination, and improvement. Hence it is that the culture of Europe was for long so churlishly and grudgingly accepted. Even now men are not wanting—and scholars, too—who affect to find in the out-worn shastras a complete satisfaction for the spiritual needs of humanity. The change which has to be effected, which is slowly going on, needs for its achievement the earnest, enthusiastic toil of a host of many-sided men, who can absorb the modern spirit without casting off their nationality. The new must be wedded to the old, blended with it in one existence, before the plastic force which is to enrich the future can find complete development. To bring about such a consummation, it is manifest that much more must be done than merely to draw or press larger numbers along in the traditional grooves. A mere increase of numbers without an enlargement of thought rather adds to the mass of prejudice through which a path has to be made towards the light. Provision must be made, and made ever more effective, for affording the appropriate nurture to the natural leaders of mental progress. It is they who, equally with the great rishis of the past, will give its peculiar stamp to the native character. The weaker men must follow in their train. Thus, to afford to native students of superior abilities the means of growing truly learned and wise, is the noblest gift that England can bestow on India when peace and order have once been secured. There is, no doubt, a great advantage in raising the general level of low intelligence by means of diffused primary instruction. Mere skill in arithmetic is a great economical benefit. But the bonds of affinity which link the genius of one nation to another, are not to be found in the ideas and feelings of a mass of mediocrities. It is in the higher regions of thought that the points of union are found; there it is that the powers are disciplined, the judgments formed, the inspirations caught, which afterwards the crowd instinctively, almost unconsciously, obey. It is by associating with the master-minds of our own and former generations that individual genius takes the bent which fits it to be the exponent of what is eternal in the thoughts that surround it. Thus, and thus only, can be formed and perfected the fit interpreters between the long-severed branches of the Aryan family.

It cannot perhaps be said with exact truth that far-reaching aims, extending to an ultimate fusion of the civilisation of the East and the West, animated the eminent men who laid the foundations of modern State education in India. But being themselves in some degree scholars, they sympathised with learning, and desired to enter into alliance with it. Looking on native society as they did, in the condition it had reached unaffected by European influences, the importance of the higher education was more strongly and immediately evident to them than that of primary instruction, which has since sometimes been made to stand in the way of vital progress. Warren Hastings, a man whose real greatness comes out the clearer from every fresh investigation, founded the Madresa, a Mahomedan college, at Calcutta in 1781. Jonathan Duncan founded the Sanskrit College at Benares in 1791. Mountstuart Elphinstone held large and liberal views about education, to which he was prepared to give effect notwithstanding the risks which might attend such a policy. His immediate successor as Commissioner of the Dekkan, Mr. Chaplin, founded the Sanskrit College at Poona in 1821. This institution was abolished, and the materials were recast in 1851. It had proved useless and barren, if not worse; and but little more could be said of the colleges at Benares and Calcutta. So long as such institutions worked on a traditional and purely indigenous basis they could but maintain an inert existence. They needed communion with the learning and philosophy of Europe, with a new science, a different history, and a different social theory, before the dry bones could live again. More recent experience has shown that a revival was quite possible, and is gradually teaching how the renewed life may become wise and fruitful for India and for mankind.

The small beginnings to which I have pointed still went farther than the State in England, in the last century, was inclined to go. Yet the sense of public responsibility for the education of the people was gradually gathering force. It was easier to spend Indian than English money on an experiment in State education; and thus it came about that India took the lead of England, by almost a generation, in providing pecuniarily, to some extent, for public instruction. By the Charter Act of 1813 the Governor-General was authorised to spend an annual sum of not less than a lakh of rupees, out of the surplus territorial revenue, on the revival and improvement of literature, the encouragement of the learned natives of India, and on "the introduction and promotion of a knowledge of the sciences among the inhabitants of the British territories in India." The aim was a generous one, but it was vaguely conceived. The true nature and extent of the obligation and of the burdens it imposed had to be learned from experience. For many years, in Bengal, the initiative in extending education was left wholly to private efforts.

Mountstuart Elphinstone, as Governor of Bombay, laid down his interpretation of the duty cast on the Indian Government in terms which involved the principles of the present system. The Government was, by means of its subsidies, to improve the teaching in native schools, to supply school-books, to encourage the lower and poorer classes to accept instruction, to establish schools for imparting European science and higher education, to provide for the publication of books on moral and physical science in the vernacular, to establish schools for teaching English as a discipline, and as a means of acquiring a knowledge of European science and learning; in the study of which the natives were to be encouraged. A beginning had already been made, and on Elphinstone's retirement a fitting memorial was raised to him in the shape of the institution out of which have since grown the Elphinstone College and School. At Poona, meanwhile, a charity fund of Rs. 35,000 a year was expended on the Sanskrit College, an institution of purely indigenous type, and from which European literature and science were jealously excluded.

In the Bombay Presidency State education proceeded for a generation on the foundation thus laid by Elphinstone. But the higher learning, being virtually left to the care of the Sanskrit College and of native scholars languished, and with it the initiatory studies to which it should have afforded a standard and stimulus. Much was done to diffuse business knowledge, and the missionary volunteers who stepped into the field of education were protected and encouraged, but the mental centre of the native community remained almost unchanged, no communion was established between cultivated Hindu minds and those of European scholars. The Sanskrit College, it was found after a long trial, "had failed of its object, had fulfilled no purpose but that of perpetuating prejudices and false systems of opinion;" without abandoning the old ruts, true progress was impossible.

In Bengal, meanwhile, arose the famous controversy on the proper basis of teaching as Oriental or English, in which the last word was for long and by many supposed to have been pronounced by Macaulay in his Minute of 1836. This is full of its author's one-sidedness and rhetorical exaggeration. But in advocating English rather than Sanskrit or Arabic he was right even in the interests of these languages and of those learned in them. What those languages contain of positive learning, science, and philosophy, though valuable for the history of the human mind, for comparison and for suggestion, yet rests on a narrow and defective view of men's mutual relations, and on a distorted and erroneous observation of physical facts. A science accepting grotesque contradictions of established truths and history, everywhere defaced by crude fable, had necessarily to be discarded. The rich grains of thought embedded in so much rubbish could be severed and saved only by the application of new standards and a newly-developed faculty of discrimination.

Still the acceptance and the spread of European thought was a slow process. One great reason for this was the indifference or dislike of the higher official class to literary culture in the natives. Even in 1852 we find Sir G. Campbell saying—

"Lord Hardinge distinguished himself by a declaration, for the encouragement of education in the Government colleges, that proficiency should lead to employment in the service of Government, which has not been and cannot be carried out, mainly because a business education is not given in those colleges, and the efficient service of Government cannot be sacrificed to the gratification of literary fancies. A young Hindu may know Milton by heart, and yet not be fit for the charge of a police station." [1]

The writer of such a passage as this evidently failed not only in sympathy with the cravings of able natives for an enlarged mental horizon, but in appreciation of the marked superiority of a well-cultivated mind even for the practical work of every-day life. It has since been discovered that as the work of administration grows more refined and difficult, the graduates of a University make the best judges and executive officers in all but the lowest grades. As to education for purposes out-

[1] Campbell, 'Modern India,' p. 198.

side this narrow circle, Sir A. Lyall has expressed the general conviction of thinking Englishmen—

"England's prime function in India is at present this: to superintend the tranquil elevation of the whole moral and intellectual standard."[1]

The wide diffusion of a colloquial knowledge of English, and a general movement of thought in matters educational, at last prepared the way for a further great advance. The Dispatch of 1854, dictated by Sir Charles Wood, was the foundation of the existing system of public education in India. The Court of Directors said: "The education we desire to see extended is that which has for its object the diffusion of the improvements, science, philosophy, and literature of Europe—in short, of European knowledge." They ordered that a graduated series of schools and colleges should be established, crowned in each Presidency by a University. The time was ripe for a great step in advance. The new system was introduced, and the Acts of the Legislature creating the Universities, passed in the year of the great Mutiny, subsist as monuments of the coolness and persistent energy of the English race.

The system of public instruction thus set on foot imitates in its outlines the English system. But it is more complete and connected in its parts, and it recognises more than the English system the duty of

[1] Sir A. Lyall, 'Asiatic Studies,' p. 305.

the State to support education in all its stages as equally important to the public welfare. The boons held out by the Government have been eagerly grasped by the people. The burden of educating a nation, though shared by the voluntary bodies, grew heavier year by year. The demand for secondary and higher education, given now in a far more effective way than formerly, continually increased. Some alarm was felt at the vast numbers of youths passing through the secondary schools to the Universities. A reaction of feeling set in amongst the European community; and it is not too much to say that now for several years any extension of higher education has by many been looked on with comparative coldness, if not positive disfavour, except when it took the shape of technical instruction. Primary education, which no doubt deserves all possible encouragement, has, it may be feared, in some instances been cried up only to cry a higher education down. Some native writers even have joined in the cry. Thus Mr. Nanjoshi, writing in 1890, says, "In the 'Self-Government Acts' adequate provision is made for elementary education, but the machinery by which the adequacy has to be judged has not been working. Hundreds of villages have yet got no schools; higher and secondary schools yet continue to be the white elephants in the department, and primary education is being starved."

There are no doubt remote villages, and there are half-savage tribes to which education has hardly penetrated; but primary instruction is now so diffused as to confer an average of three or four years' schooling on every available boy of the school-going age. The education of girls has lagged far behind, but its progress in numbers is now not less rapid than that of boys.

It is unquestionably an evil when secondary education, still more when University education, so to speak, outruns primary instruction. Improved faculty, enlarged productiveness, in the lower strata of society ought to furnish the material on which its higher members work. There is no great need for a large multiplication of secondary schools and of colleges affiliated to the Universities, but there is need for access to them being made easy to ability, and great need for their teaching being raised and widened, if those who pass through them and become the intellectual leaders of India are to be equal to their high calling, and are to take a part honourable to themselves and their nation in the creation of an imperial spirit which shall supersede all ideas of severance, and further that fusion of the philosophies of the East and West to which we may now look most hopefully for the moral and intellectual advance of mankind.

The means at the disposal of Government for purposes of education in a country where the material edifice of modern civilisation has to be built up in one or two generations are necessarily scanty. In the Bombay Presidency, where, perhaps, public education has been the most earnestly pushed forward, one-sixteenth of the land-tax is handed over to the local boards, and these are required to expend one-third of the amount on elementary education. Municipalities must provide for primary instruction, and may provide middle and higher schools. The Government, several years ago, engaged, to the extent of its means, to pay one-third of the cost of the schools which should be thus established; but the hunger for education has exceeded the resources available to satisfy it. The municipalities are so alive to the advantages of a comparatively advanced education that they desire to set up secondary schools, to which the Government is unable to contribute. The primary schools are treated as a first charge on the public resources, whether local or provincial; and secondary schools have in some cases even been suppressed. Where they gave but a meagre feast of "cram" without true enlargement or elevation, the result is not perhaps much to be deplored; but the money thus saved would be best expended on making the higher education in all its stages more worthy of that name. The tests for admission to the secondary schools and classes should be more strict. The teaching should be more individual and formative, the leaving examinations qualifying for appearance at the entrance examinations of the University should be far more exacting than they are. Not more than half of those pronounced fit by the schoolmasters succeed in the entrance examination, which, however, itself still admits many whom Nature will never allow to be scholars. The supply of professional men will not fail, and a mass of dull graduates crammed with formulus which they cannot assimilate, are a mere dead-weight on the community. The eagerness which everywhere subsists for secondary education should be satisfied in another way, the duty of the local bodies should be fulfilled in another way, than by an indiscriminate establishment of new schools which, being ill-supported, must needs be inefficient. Every town community qualified for municipal rank, say of 5,000 inhabitants or upwards, should be required to provide by a small rate for the subsistence by stipends of one student at a central secondary school for each 2,000 of its population, and for one student at an Arts College or a professional college for each 4,000 of the population. The students sent up should be subject to proper tests, and the fees should be payable whether students were provided or not. This would be a great and systematic extension of the scheme of stipends already acted on by some municipalities. It could readily be extended to the rural local boards. The increase of individual local burdens would be almost imperceptible, and the high schools and colleges, enriched by additional contributions, could enlarge and improve their standards of education and their teaching staff.

Sir Richard Temple, writing in 1880,[1] said—

"The fact that the Government in India maintains colleges of its own at all is the subject of complaint in some quarters. It is urged that the efforts of the State in this direction should be confined to making grants-in-aid to the colleges belonging to private societies; that these private colleges are suffering from the competition of the Government colleges; and that the Government colleges at the Presidency cities of Calcutta, Madras, and Bombay ought to be closed."

Yet, as he further observes—

"The authorities at the Presidency colleges do not attempt to undermine the missionary colleges by charging town fees; on the contrary, they charge somewhat higher fees than those of any private institutions."

The fact is, that the greatly increased energy of teaching in the Government institutions, and the attraction of Government scholarships, had begun to draw off a large proportion of the promising pupils from the institutions of the missionary bodies. It may be true also that the now highly-organised and compact Educational Departments looked with

[1] India in 1880, p. 147.

some dislike or disdain on their humbler rivals; but that any unfairness was shown in the dispensation of the Government grants was never proved. The Government had, in truth, grown only too anxious to shift the burden of education as much as possible from its own shoulders. It set on foot the Educational Commission, which, after an elaborate enquiry in all parts of India, presented its Report in 1882. This recommended a far-reaching transfer of education from the Government to private control. Secondary education, the Commission said, ought to be gradually transferred to native management; it should no longer be the concern of Government when once Government could withdraw without lowering the standards. Thus the managing bodies which had proved unequal to compete with the Government schools on equal terms were to supersede them, with all their chances of lax management, defective teaching, and the impossibility of personal adaptation which attends small organisations as compared with great ones. Outside the Government schools and colleges the higher education of India was virtually in the hands of the various missionary bodies; and to them first-rate teaching of secular subjects could not, perhaps ought not, to be the principal object. In spite of ability, devotion, and force of character in individual cases, it is even more true for India than for a European state, that "a public system of schools is indispensable in modern communities," if only for this, that "of public schools you can take guarantees, of private schools you cannot." You can examine the pupils, and regulate your grant-in-aid according to the results; but you cannot maintain the same scientific methods, the same ideal of attainments, the same superiority in the body of teachers, as where they are chosen purely on grounds of scholarship and competence, are independent of the pupils and their parents, and animated with the emulous spirit of a great body free to strive, and always striving from good to better in system and practice.

The recommendations of the Educational Commission pointed to a considerable saving to the Government. Private effort was ready to take up high education, and the Government wished as far as possible to transfer it. Even "Board schools and municipal schools," the Government of India said, "are not private institutions in the sense contemplated by the Commission. What is meant is a transfer of the Government schools and Board schools to the hands of trustees in order to set free funds for the extension of education in other directions." In giving effect to the principles thus indicated, the Educational Department have "retired in a somewhat wholesale manner from the conduct of secondary schools," in spite of the grave objections already noted, and others arising from the necessity of preserving a balance amongst opposing races and sects. When private bodies of natives take up the work of education there is the further danger of its being perverted to stimulate separatist sentiments and foster national pride in forms that may prove politically mischievous. Free criticism is what every Government, founded in any degree on British principles, must be content to submit to, but the function of public censors does not afford a safe and wholesome exercise for schoolboys, or even for their teachers. A uniform acceptance of the system under which they live, loyalty to the Throne, and proud satisfaction in forming part of a great progressive empire, are highly favourable, by the lofty calm which they tend to produce, to both mental and moral enlargement. Indolence on the part of Government, or a short-sighted indifference to the great opportunities it enjoys, may well prove the source of infinite troubles in a not distant future.

Between 1883 and 1886 there was a diminution from 282 to 230 of the English secondary schools under State management in British India, while those under Local Boards and municipalities increased from 281 to 342. "Private trustees" have as yet barely come into the field. The missionary schools and colleges only are growing in number and usefulness. The somewhat precipitate course that secondary education was taking was pointed out to the Government of India, but the result was only to draw from it a declaration in 1888 that, "In educational, as in all other matters, it is the policy of the Government of India to avoid entering into competition with private enterprise." Its activity was, therefore, to be limited "to helping, by reasonable subventions, the operation of independent institutions." It would "maintain but a few schools," in order "to afford a standard." It was laid down that "expenditure on Government educational institutions should be a constantly diminishing quantity, provided there is the assurance that the ground abandoned by Government will be occupied by local effort." There was even to be "a contraction in the numbers educated, especially in the high schools and colleges still maintained by Government."

The Administration Report of 1888-89 shows that this resolution of the Government of India was generally disapproved by the organs of public opinion. They condemned as a retrograde step the transfer of the higher education to private bodies, not accepting the principle that the education of a people was like a manufacturing business, in which Government ought not to compete with private enterprise, or not seeing the enterprise with which it was to compete. They agreed rather with the views of Macaulay, so vigorously expressed on a similar subject in 1847.

"We have just come victorious out of a long and fierce contest for the liberty of trade. While that contest was undecided, much was said and written about the advantages of free competition, and about the danger of suffering the State to regulate matters which should be left to individuals. There has consequently arisen in the minds of persons who are led by words, and who are little in the habit of making distinctions, a disposition to apply to polititical questions and moral questions principles which are sound only when applied to commercial questions. These people, not content with having forced the Government to surrender a province wrongfully usurped, now wish to wrest from the Government a domain held by a right which was never before questioned, and which cannot be questioned with the smallest show of reason. "If," they say, "free competition is a good thing in trade, it must surely be a good thing in education. The supply of other commodities—of sugar, for example—is left to adjust itself to the demand; and the consequence is that we are better supplied with sugar than if the Government undertook to supply us. Why then should we doubt that the supply of instruction will, without the intervention of the Government, be found equal to the demand?" Never was there a more false analogy."

The policy of withdrawal, however, has been steadily pursued. In Madras, in 1888-89, there were 147 upper secondary schools, but of these only four remained, which were directly supported and controlled by Government. In other provinces a similar process has gone on, though on a less sweeping scale. There has been a vast extension of secondary education in the last ten years, but the charge to Government has decreased, the augmented expenses being defrayed chiefly by increased fees. Nothing could testify more strongly than this to the eagerness of the people for advanced education. They desire English education in preference to vernacular; but, judging by numbers, they desire instruction in the classical languages, and especially in Sanskrit, still fifty per cent. more than in English. It is evident that there is room now for an enlargement of the basis of Sanskrit study; it should no longer remain isolated, but should be taught and learned in connection with all that may be gained through English of the European ways of facing the same problems which Sanskrit literature presents and strives to solve. It is not unworthy of the most powerful Government that it should respond to the nobler cravings of its subjects, and the expansion of the classical teaching need not involve any such expense as would materially disturb the balance between the outlay on secondary and on primary education. The youths receiving secondary education amount, after all, to only some five per cent. of the whole number recorded as under instruction in India. The students in colleges amount to no more than one per cent. In England the proportion is twice as great; in a German State four or five times as great, of youths under secondary instruction. In a German town, indeed, from a third to a half of the children are in the higher schools; but in Germany it is everywhere recognised, in direct opposition to the principle announced by the Government of India, that the State is more especially interested in the higher education, the town or locality in the lower. The contributions of Government are regulated accordingly.

In 1890–91 the expenditure of the Government of Bombay in aid of secondary schools is set down as Rs. 10,230 on secondary schools under municipalities against Rs. 27,403 contributed by the municipal funds, and Rs. 27,348 obtained from fees. This is, of course, far from representing the whole case, since Rs. 125,000 were expended on secondary schools managed directly by Government. But even here fees were levied to the amount of Rs. 183,000. For aided secondary schools under private management Government contributed Rs. 190,000 towards an aggregate expenditure of Rs. 700,000. The fees produced Rs. 275,000, and the endowments about Rs. 228,000. To secondary schools managed by District Local Boards the Government contributed but Rs. 391 out of about Rs. 5,000. To the Government secondary schools the municipalities contributed but Rs. 6,700 and the Local Boards nothing. These figures show that the Bombay Government has not indeed wholly withdrawn from its care of secondary education, but they show too that the municipalities are but little encouraged in their efforts to maintain higher education, and that the public contributions all round are meagre and insufficient. So far from being pampered, secondary education is starved, except in so far as it is sustained by the payments of fees, and these in India are extracted mainly from a needy, half-famished class, having as strong a claim as any to the public aid in qualifying their children for their future callings. In the native States under Bombay the total expenditure on secondary education was Rs. 190,000, and of this the States contributed Rs. 134,000. Admitting then the claims of primary instruction, it may fairly be contended that even in Bombay secondary education, so greedily sought and readily paid for by the people, may properly ask such support from the State as shall raise it to the highest efficiency, and by means of bursaries bring it within reach of every boy of adequate capacity and promise. If all India is taken into view the case is no better, perhaps worse than in Bombay. Between 1881 and 1885 the total cost of secondary instruction for boys rose from forty-four to sixty-four lakhs of rupees, while the Government contributions actually diminished from Rs. 1,596,000 to Rs. 1,518,000. In Madras in 1888–89 there were 147 high schools, with some 26,000 pupils. But of these forty-seven were unaided, and, of course, uncontrolled; sixty-eight were aided;

twenty-eight were Local Board schools, and only four directly supported and controlled by Government.

In University education the retrogression of Government has been marked in 1889–90 by reducing the staff of European professors at the Hooghley College, and by placing the Krishnagur and Rajashaha Colleges under a European principal of the subordinate educational service, assisted by graduates of the Calcutta University. The education at these institutions may possibly not be seriously and immediately impaired by the changes in the staff; but there is, at least, a risk of deterioration. The students in the Bengal Colleges went on meanwhile increasing, while the cost of each to Government fell by about twenty per cent. Economy was further attained by refusing grants-in-aid to 413 secondary schools in 1889–90, which was followed in 1890–91 by a decline of 2,000 in the number of pupils in these establishments, though the number of schools increased. In the Panjab, of six colleges, only one remained under Government control in 1890-91. The control of University education, of which the Government is divesting itself, is not as yet passing in any large measure into native hands. In Madras in 1887–88, of eleven first-class colleges teaching the course up to the B.A. degree, seven were aided colleges, six maintained by missionary bodies, and one the Doveton (Protestant) College. Three high schools, it is said, became second-grade colleges, teaching up to the first examination in arts, and three, it is further said, are under native committees. There is one college of higher rank, founded by the Maharajah of Vizianagram; but the most completely developed, and perhaps the only fully developed college under purely native management in India, is the Fergusson College at Poona. The college at Aligarh is a native foundation, but it is under a European principal. It is the missionaries who thus far are taking the place of Government, and the readiness with which their teaching is accepted proves the intense desire of the people for high education. There is no reason to doubt that the missionary colleges do their work efficiently; their students take honours in the University examinations. Yet secular instruction is not the aim of their being, and Sir A. Croft remarks of Bengal, in 1888–89, that the superiority of the Government colleges was fully maintained.

The institution of the science degrees in the Indian Universities, or the introduction of the science subjects into the course for B.A., produced a certain movement from the literary to the science course. In Madras, in 1887–8, there was a transfer of about thirty per cent. of candidates from languages to the various "optional" or selected subjects. The extension of professional openings and professional studies will, it may be hoped, continue to attract many students to physical science;

but, in spite of the general success of the candidates for degrees taking up the optional subjects, they have of late declined in numbers from year to year. Sir A. Croft observes that in the unaided colleges science is virtually no longer taught. The strong natural bent of the people of Bengal has prevailed against all inducements.

In Bombay the impetus given under Lord Reay's administration to technical teaching has not yet lost any of its force. It is maintained with liberality, the expenditure in 1890–91 having risen from 89,000 rupees to 123,000 rupees contributed by Government. Literary education and technical training go on *pari passu*, though pursued generally by quite different classes of students. But training for practical ends is sought in the Victoria Jubilee Technical Institute, and in the classes of the Poona College of Science. In the University the old order of studies still maintains its predominance. The number of students taking up the classical languages does not decline, and the general interest of native society in the Sanskrit literature grows more pronounced as it grows more enlightened. But while the demand for a higher and more complete teaching is thus growing, the means of teaching, even where they have not been lessened, have not been allowed to increase. There would seem, as Sir A. Croft reported in 1888, to be "room for a great development of the highest form of education, of the value of which to its possessors and to the State there can be little doubt;" but the Government colleges, which could best impart the highest instruction, are bound down to tasks of a lower order by the insufficiency of their staffs. Mr. Wordsworth, the Principal of the Elphinstone College, reports: "If no additions are to be made, the work of preparing youths for the previous examinations should be carried on in the high schools or provincial colleges, and this college be open only to students preparing for the higher examinations. With our existing staff we could teach these pretty effectually, and include in our course some lectures for those reading for the degree of M.A." It is evident, then, that, as at present constituted and manned, the Government colleges fall short of giving that highest instruction without which all the lower teaching must more or less fail to produce a creative, reproductive intelligence. It is only to Government agency that we can look for this highest teaching; and for a due balance of effort and development amongst the several classes of instruction it is indispensable.

It has already been pointed out, in the inaugural address of the eminent President of this Congress, how the study of Sanskrit has, in the past generation, added to the history of the human mind and of human institutions. It is taking an ever-widening place in the field of literature and history, and the facts and thoughts which it presents claim more and more an equal place beside those furnished by the more familiar literature of ancient and modern Europe. For India a correct appreciation of the teachings of its literature is of inestimable importance. In no other country is the present so deeply rooted in the past; in none are existing institutions, beliefs, and manners so unintelligible, except by reference to their origin in a remote antiquity. The search for what this far past has to reveal, the interpretation of what it has to tell, ought to be, must be in great part, the work of native scholars. But just as the treasures of Sanskrit are now found indispensable by the European scholar to a complete survey of human progress, so must the native student be furnished with an ample armament of general culture, with European learning and European methods of investigation, if he is to discover and appreciate the golden ore in the Eastern mines of learning. He must bear a torch of European criticism if he is to draw from his native stores matter that will be accepted as a true addition to the wealth of mankind. He it is who has to take up those elements of civilisation which Europe offers, and present them in shapes which his countrymen can assimilate, and through them find their way into the great march of modern progress. A stunted and merely Asiatic culture will for such a purpose be almost useless. Of Sanskrit, as of many other things, it may be said that to know it alone is but to half know it, and recent history demonstrates that its study cannot really flourish except when it grows side by side with a free and generous culture in the widest sense.

The few purely Oriental colleges that have survived in India have been described as "mere remnants of old institutions, designed for the cultivation of the classical learning of the Hindus and Mahomedans, especially as bearing on their religion, laws, and customs." Only three of these colleges survive: the Sanskrit department of the college at Benares; the Oriental department of the Canning College at Lucknow, and the Oriental college at Lahore. There is also the Madrasa at Calcutta, but this has become merely a second-grade college. Its standard in Arabic is not prescribed by any University, and its literary energy stands almost at zero. The Oriental department of the Canning College has about ninety students, of whom the majority are Mahomedans. They are examined by the Punjab University for its Oriental titles, but not for ordinary degrees. The Calcutta Sanskrit College now instructs classes for the first examination in Arts. Some half-dozen or so of students may be found reading Sanskrit for the degree of M.A. The Sanskrit department of the College at Benares presents a much better figure. It has about 460 students. Proficiency is rewarded by Oriental titles. In the

Anglo-Sanskrit department there are about fifty students, mostly pundits of advanced years. The crowd of Brahmins, who in former days taught Sanskrit to thousands of disciples from all parts of India, has vanished. The ancient interest in the study has died out, the newer interest seeks other ways of satisfaction. The Benares students, as may well be supposed, devote themselves to learning with great zeal and assiduity; and the knowledge they acquire is, in a narrow way, solid and complete. Yet we learn that outside "mathematics and astronomy, taught by translations from English, the teaching moves entirely in the old grooves. What we should call a critical knowledge of the language is scarcely to be found." The Anglo-Sanskrit department, opened, or reopened, in 1884, has not as yet had time to produce any material effect.

We could not gather from these examples that Sanskrit, standing alone and as a law unto itself, was capable of doing much for the mental enrichment of modern India, or even of long maintaining itself as a subject of general serious study. The Oriental College at Lahore was started with wider aims and a more promising announcement of studies. "It cultivates the Oriental classical languages along with the higher branches of European knowledge through the vernaculars. . . . Students are thus prepared for examination in arts, medicine, and engineering." . . . The chief object of the students is not the acquisition of general knowledge, but the advanced study of the Eastern classics. . . . The higher training in the classics enables us to attract classes who have a desire for Eastern but none for Western learning, and to insist on the acquisition of a certain amount of more general knowledge—that required for the entrance examination of the Oriental Faculty. . . . We hope gradually to lead our students to follow the course for degrees rather than that for titles."

The Punjab College was made a University in 1882. It was intended to be Oriental in spirit and character without being confined to the study of Oriental learning and languages. The examinations in Arts are held not only in English but in the vernacular languages, and an Oriental Faculty examines for special degrees in Oriental classics. An institution resting on such broad and liberal ideas ought *à priori* to have achieved a great success. It may be presumed to have done for Sanskrit and Arabic all that could be done by merely Oriental methods. These were carried so far that astronomy was taught for some time according to the Ptolemaic system, as adopted by the Arabians. An investigation into the working of the institution was held in 1885–86, and this "brought to light the extraordinary condition of affairs that all the students who were attending the college and school were stipendaries, with the exception of forty-six, who were in expectation of receiving stipends." This gave occasion to some very caustic comments on the part of the Lieutenant-Governor, who found that students' stipends had been drawn for eight, ten, and even fourteen years. "With regard to the scope of the pretensions and the operations of the Oriental College and School," the Sub-Committee found that they were "altogether out of proportion to the available means, teaching power, and appliances." The Sub-Committee state, "There are, at present, no classes in Hindu and Mahomedan law. As regards the medical classes, it was found that the only instruction given was half an hour a day in the study of ancient Sanskrit, or Arabic medical books." Yet the Oriental classics, it was reported, were taught up to a high standard, and science and general knowledge were well conveyed through the vernacular. The purely artificial character of the Institution was proved by the fact that, as compared with an expenditure by Government of Rs. 25,447, only Rs. 578 were realised from fees.

It seems to result from this examination of all the available instances, that Oriental education, on a purely Oriental basis in India, has not quite succeeded, even when tried under the most favourable conditions. It is equally evident that there is an insufficient provision for high University education. In 1885–6, as Sir Alfred Croft points out, only twelve colleges in all India prepared candidates successfully for the degree of M.A. "If the instruction were provided, there would probably be no lack of students to take advantage of it." It ought to be provided, and especially in Sanskrit, as the completion and the crown of a thorough and comprehensive course of general study—linked closely on to the whole body of University teaching. It is as important to the students of to-day, who are to be the teachers of the future, as a knowledge of precedents is to the English lawyer. It should be taught, if necessary, more intensively rather than extensively. It is dear to the people, the key by which the riddle of their existence is solved, a means whereby the two great masses of British subjects can at length meet upon a common ground of thought.

I have pointed to the fact that the system of public education in India was similar in its main outlines to the English system. It was well to start from a known platform, but the English plan was obviously but a fragment of a complete system. It provided only for the simplest rudimentary instruction as a public care. The State education of India is in this respect immensely ahead of it, and yet this, especially in recent years, has been obstructed and embarrassed by a tangle of notions of British growth, grown obsolete, in a great measure, even in the United Kingdom, and wholly inapplicable to a country of such widely different conditions as India.

The statesman of India should be enlightened, not enslaved, by the example of this country.

> "Not clinging to an ancient saw,
> Not mastered by a modern term."

Piercing through circumstances to principles he should discern that the higher and the highest education he can bestow is the perpetual want of India until it be satisfied, and that the interest of England is beyond all measure concerned in the shape and direction given to the growing and aspiring intellect of the great dependency.

The secondary schools in India have this advantage over the endowed schools in England, that they are subject to regular and searching examination. They form a part of the system inspected and controlled by the Education Department. In England, on the other hand, when the Charity Commissioners have once framed a scheme for a school, and set it going, it is thenceforward left very much to itself. It does not come within the visitations of the Inspectors of Schools, because it is not a primary aided school; the Charity Commissioners have no authority to appoint inspectors or exercise superintendence. Hence they have no official means of testing either the soundness of their schemes or the intelligence and zeal with which they are carried out by the governing bodies. Nor can the Charity Commissioners find out with any certainty where a want of secondary education is most felt, and how for each locality it may best be supplied. Wales and Scotland are in this respect distinctly in advance of England. In England the State does not found high schools or help, or even inspect them. They are found in some places where they are almost thrown away. In others they exist not where they are most needed, or exist only through private enterprise or benevolence. There are some scholarships linking the primary to the secondary schools, and this is a point at which the Charity Commissioners aim in their schemes for reorganising educational foundations; but there is an absolute want of continuity and system as between the lower and the higher education. The State looks after the former; the latter, equally important, is left almost to chance. India, in the outline, at least, of its educational system, approaches the completeness of Germany. There is a regular gradation of schools and of studies from the lowest to the highest, and to the University. Voluntary bodies who have established schools and colleges receive grants in aid on terms which place them on an equality with the Government institutions, and which are perfectly satisfactory to them. They provide instruction in many cases at lower rates and with more consideration for individual cases than the purely public institutions. A poor boy of unusual ability knows exactly what opportunities are open to him, what line he has to take in order to make his way to a University degree;

and there are aids enough on the way in the shape of Government and municipal scholarships to encourage him in diligence. The plan of Indian public education is not ill laid down. What it wants is enrichment, enlargement, the capacity and means to cultivate the best abilities, to turn out and preserve to learning a larger—a much larger—proportion of distinguished men among the host of mediocrites. But it needs, too, a recognition of the principle thoroughly accepted in Germany, that the higher the scale of education the wider the region instructed in it. Thus the State should contribute a larger proportion to the secondary than to the primary school. In India it is generally just the reverse. In England secondary education is left to take care of itself. The very wealth of endowments with which the community has been enriched by the munificence of past generations has in recent years stood in the way of a systematic progress of scholars from the lowest to the highest rung of the educational ladder. Many of our great foundations date from an earlier period, but the sixteenth century was particularly fruitful in grammar-schools. It was a time when men's minds were greatly and nobly stirred, a time of rising prices, of prosperity for the middle classes, and of confidence in the future. The endowments took generally the form of dedications of land, which were specially appropriate for large towns, because the value of the land would increase with the growth of population, and of children needing instruction. The stream of benevolence, though lessened in proportion to the nation's wealth, has never ceased to flow, but many new objects have arisen, and new means of elementary education have come into existence on lines different from those of earlier times. A generous education was in the times following the revival of learning recognised as the only education. Instruction aimed at learning, as learning was then conceived; but the practical needs of active life were little cared for by the grammar-school master, and the demand for immediately useful instruction, even on a very low level, gave rise to the private adventure schools in which the mass of middle-class Englishmen have been brought up.

No country shows more than England the impoverishment which the lower everyday studies suffer through a divorce from the higher. While classical and philosophical learning has kept on the old lines, sharing fairly in the general movement of European thought, though suffering by its partial severance from the great active interests of the nation, the exigencies of daily life amongst a lower, rougher class have been met by a rude rule-of-thumb education, or rather instruction, supplying in a fragmentary unorganised way such scraps of practical accomplishments as were indispensable for purposes of business. There is neither the systematic discipline imposed on the teachers and learners of the classical languages nor is teaching based on a thorough study of human faculties and human growth, and working on this foundation towards a gymnastic of the mind, which shall open wider and strengthen it in such a sequence of training as may produce the maximum of energy and flexibility in the whole sphere of effort and invention within which the intended occupations are embraced.

Individual genius of course triumphs in England, as everywhere, over the obstacle of unfavourable surroundings, but in England perhaps more than anywhere capacity goes to waste through want of cultivation. Recent years no doubt have seen great efforts made by the Charity Commissioners to make the educational endowments which abound in some parts of the country available for carrying on youths of exceptional promise from one stage to another of education. The existence even of such possibilities for ability and diligence is not generally known. There is a complete absence of a system connecting the lower with the higher schools, and with the Universities. There may incidentally and occasionally be some gain in leaving a leaven of high intelligence, even though uncultivated, to work amongst the masses; but this is not to be compared in value, socially or politically, with a continuous and regular movement upwards, bringing home to the poor and ignorant, that for them as for others—for their sons, at any rate—there is a free career open to ability. A chain of common intellectual interests, binding the different orders of the community together, is not less important in view of the rising problems of the future, than the political and religious connections which counteract the severing influence of differences of means. Now, in the matter of gradation and co-ordination in its educational system, India is distinctly in advance of England. Scotland and Wales will bear comparison with India, as they take greatly the lead of England, but in any criticism of the Indian Educational Department, it must be borne in mind that, with limited means, and with enormous difficulties to contend against, the Government has placed instruction, and the highest instruction, fairly within the reach of every youth of ability who chooses to strive for it.

By the Welsh Intermediate Education Act of 1889, provision is made for an Education Committee for each county. The Committee is to submit to the Charity Commissioners a scheme for the intermediary and technical education of the country, and for the use of existing endowments. The County Council may provide for the scheme out of the county rate, with a condition for its own representation on the governing board. The scheme has to be dealt with and put in operation by the Charity Commissioners, like one for an endowed school. Provision is thus made for a complete scheme of secondary schools if only the County Councils will vote the requisite funds. The extra rate for this purpose must not exceed a halfpenny in the pound. To the sum thus raised may be added an equal sum from the Treasury, on condition of the schools being maintained in an efficient state. The schemes proposed must be approved by the Charity Commissioners, which it may be hoped will prevent any degradation of the existing means, slender as they are, of higher instruction.

In Scotland, secondary education has in some way been provided for in the ordinary schools during the last two centuries. There are many more endowments than in Wales, though not so many as in England. A power of rating not only for lower but for higher class schools, was given by the legislation of twenty years ago. It was found by experience that enough had not been done for secondary education, and further arrangements had to be made, but the problem presented itself under far more favourable conditions than elsewhere.

By a recent order of the Scottish Education Commission of the Privy Council, a representative Committee will be formed for every county.

It will report on the existing means of higher education in each county in Scotland.

It will name the schools fitted for an additional provision, and the school districts where new schools are needed. It will say whether any secondary school, not being a higher-class public school under the Act of 1872, is eligible for a share in the grant.

It will consider any proposal submitted by the County Council for promoting technical education in connection with secondary education by means of funds at its disposal.

There are similar provisions for the great burghs of Edinburgh, Glasgow, Aberdeen, and Dundee.

The allowances are £3 a head for average of boys above 13 who have passed Standard VI.; £6 a head for children who, having been for three years in a public or State-aided school, have passed Standard VI., and such further examination as may be prescribed to test their fitness for secondary education; £2 a head for those under 13 who have passed Standard VI.; to State-aided schools making provision for higher education, £1 a head for each pupil passing the third stage of a special subject deemed secondary, and £3 for each who then remains a year learning secondary subjects.

Suitable buildings must be provided and the curriculum must be approved as conditions of the aforesaid grants.

The continuation of the grant is conditional on annual approval by the County Committee or Burgh Committee and Scottish Education Department of the work of the schools.

I have pointed already to the earnest and widely-spread desire for secondary education which prevails in India. In the great towns which are the centres of industrial activity the craving for technical instruction is no less vigorous. The objects properly included in secondary and in technical education are very well indicated in Section 17 of the Welsh Act already referred to. It is almost a disgrace to great cities of the empire like Calcutta, Madras, and Bombay if they do not profit by the examples which have been set them by the chief towns of the United Kingdom, and, with the aid which they may most reasonably claim, establish secondary schools on a large and liberal scale. If their inhabitants in the next generation are to retain their place in the world of intellect and of material prosperity, learning and science and the applications of science must be assiduously studied. A truly corporate spirit ought to manifest itself in all ways in which, as in this, combined and co-ordinated action is immeasurably more efficient than individual effort. Offers of private endowments should be met in a generous spirit, and the Government thus shamed, if necessary, into an equal liberality. Every populous municipality in India should strive to place itself on the level of Edinburgh or Dundee, and make secondary instruction in learning and in industrial arts one of the main aims of its corporate existence. In some of the municipalities below the first rank the requisite spirit exists; in the greatest it may be feared a less noble ambition or a greater stinginess prevails. But by one means or another, from one source or another, provision must be made for keeping the Indian scholar and the Indian artificer or captain of labour abreast of the general line of progress if the gains of to-day are to be preserved, and positive retrogression is to be avoided.

The mofussil or rural districts of India are now almost everywhere brought under the control of local boards established under the impulse given by Lord Ripon's administration. These may, for our present purpose, be compared with the County Councils of the United Kingdom. Wherever, within the bounds of a zilla, the want of secondary education of either class has become distinctly felt, a way should be provided on the Welsh or the Scottish model for the constitution of a local educational council or committee, and for the establishment of such secondary schools on such a footing as may be expedient. The local boards should be invested with a power of rating within modest limits for this special purpose, and the provincial Government should be empowered or required to supplement the rate in each case with an equal sum from the general provincial revenues up to an aggregate settled quinquennially by the Imperial Government. The schemes would differ materially for different districts. It may be feared that in some apathy, or the dread even of a slightly increased fiscal burden, would prevent any universal demand for higher instruction from arising. In such cases it should be open to any substantial portion of the community to make the requisite demand, and to Government to act on such demand. The contribution from the provincial revenue would be a sufficient check on hasty assent. The principle of a local provision, compulsory for primary instruction, discretionary for secondary education, is already embodied in the law, but two further steps are necessary, or at least desirable: (1) The constitution of an Educational Commission on the Scottish system; and (2) a power to enforce action in favour of higher instruction when necessary. Add to these a uniform contribution by Government, and then the machinery would be complete. At present the Government in Bombay desires to help local boards to the extent of one-third of the cost of elementary education, but its means, like those of the local boards, are insufficient. They could be found and would be found in the quinquennial fiscal contract between the provincial and the Imperial Governments if a statutory duty were imposed on the former to aid local communities commensurately with their willingness to tax themselves both for primary and for secondary education. In most municipalities of Western India a special education rate would be least unpalatable when devoted to the purpose of higher instruction, in a liberal sense, but with due regard to the specific wants of the population. It has, indeed, been found necessary to check a municipality's contribution, and official congratulations have been uttered over municipalities' parsimony in this direction, as leaving more available for primary instruction.

Considering the position of England as the mistress of India, and the fact that Her Majesty rules over six Asiatics for one subject of European blood, the provision made in England for the encouragement of Oriental learning is of a mean and unworthy kind. The able young men who crowd our Universities, looking anxiously forward for a career, see that, except by great good fortune, to turn to Sanskrit or Arabic, instead of Greek and Latin, would be to ruin their prospects, to place themselves on a low level of means and comfort, for all their lives. India could afford something, England could afford much, towards remedying this evil, and making English Orientalists as numerous and productive, let us say, as those of Germany. In the disposal of offices that require Oriental learning, the Universities and other learned bodies would do well to give a preference to men who, by long residence in India, have gained a living acquaintance with its literature as it lives and works in the mind of the people. Native scholars of distinguished erudition should be invited and induced to take up their residence, and to work and lecture for a longer or shorter period in the United Kingdom. Some young

Englishmen of unusual zeal and promise should be sent to complete their studies at Benares. Such supplementary measures as these would complete and crown the improved development of learning in India. They would bring the metropolitan country into closer relation with its great dependency; they would do something to correct the superciliousness which springs from ignorance, and to promote that communion of thought and feeling, without which a true and all-pervading unity of imperial spirit is all but impossible.

In India, as has been done in Egypt, a large sum might be obtained for Sanskrit education out of the numerous religious endowments, without any departure from their main purpose. In some cases which have come into the Courts new schemes for the administration of the charities have been framed, and in the place of large additions to genuine places and to the crowd of mendicants to be fed gratuitously, provision has been made for the establishment and extension of schools. An Act was passed by the legislation a couple of years ago under which the Government can in many cases do even more efficiently what the Courts have sometimes done. In the present state of feeling of the native community in India, no applications of charitable funds would be more acceptable than those by which education should be extended; and if this extension should, even in part, take the shape of placing the study of Sanskrit and of Arabic on a high and scholarly basis, it would everywhere be taken as a sign of true interest and sympathy, and do much to endear their rulers to the Hindu and Mahomedan subjects of Her Majesty. Many opulent natives of India—chiefs and others—feel a deep religious, as well as a social and benevolent, interest in the higher education of their countrymen. We have only to look at the long list of endowments conferred on the University of Bombay during its one generation of existence, to see that a generous desire to aid scholarship is very widely diffused. It is indeed the opinion of some who know the University well, that there are in proportion scholarships enough, and that more good can now be done by adding to the general fund of the University than by creating additional prizes. But all will, I think, concur, when I commend to the attention of wealthy and patriotic men the founding of lectureships and scholarships constituted specially for the pursuit of original research, and for widening and deepening the foundations on which the Indian, and especially Sanskrit, learning of the future is to be built. The aim should be to make native scholars not only complete masters of their own sacred language, but masters also of the general learning and philosophy, without which their special acquirements must lose half their value.

If the several means of governmental corporate

and individual action which I have indicated should be brought to bear energetically but judiciously on Indian students, the result in a generation would be a rise in the quality of native education as remarkable as its wide extension during our own time. Whether in those active pursuits which call for a large share of physical energy the Hindus will ever quite equal Europeans may reasonably be doubted; but in learning and speculation they may certainly expect to produce some great masters from among the multitude who are ready to become submissive and earnest disciples.

In dwelling as I have done on the duty and the means of enlarging and elevating the native learning of India, I would not be understood as advocating any indiscriminate multiplication of the mere pass-men who take up Sanskrit or Persian as their classical language for the bachelor's degree. The aim should be rather to increase the depth and fulness of learning than to add to the crowd of half-trained scholars. The tasks and traditions of the Hindus tend always to throw an excessive number of competitors into the ranks of those who seek literary employment. Thousands become ill-educated scholars merely because this is their hereditary calling, and they have not energy to strike into a new career. These numerous ineffectives lower the general level of aspiration even amongst those who do better. They should be to a large extent excluded from the career of learning by severer tests applied at an early stage, and, as far as possible, other careers should be opened for them. The sluggish and incapable must needs be comparative failures in any line whatever, but many who have no literary gift might succeed as engineers, as builders, carpenters and machinists. The appliances of advanced mechanical art have as yet been but little brought to bear on the construction of houses in Indian cities. Sanitation is in its infancy; sound and pure art is but little employed by the wealthy commercial classes in the embellishment of their dwellings. In every direction there are calls for the increased application of science and the industrial arts to improve the comfort and beauty of human life. A somewhat severe code of building laws and sanitary regulations would not only improve the physical well-being of the people, but would open out occupation for a multitude of specialists and experts who would thus be drawn off from the too-crowded field of literary work. Thus the material and the intellectual improvement of the people would be directly advanced by the same measures which would gradually break down the anti-economical restrictions of such employments and wasteful modes of production.

In pointing out the shortcomings of the Sanskrit College at Benares, its principal, Dr. Thibaut, adds that the English colleges have done very little for the promotion of Sanskrit scholarship. This cannot be accepted as correct without a large qualification as applied to the colleges of the Bombay Presidency. These have produced men like Messrs. Bhándárkar, Pandit, and Telang, who know well how to employ the critical methods of European scholarship. They are able to hold their own in contests with the most advanced European scholars in matters controverted amongst them. The Bombay Sanskrit Series is a most creditable evidence in several of its productions that native scholarship,[1] while characterised by all

[1] *Publications by Natives in Bombay.*

I. S. P. Pandit:—

(1) 'Edition of the Rághuvainsà,' 3 Nros. Bo. S. S.
(2) 'Edition of the Mâlavikâgnimitra' (No. 1, two editions). Bo. S. S.
(3) 'Edition of the Vikramorveśî' (No. 1, two editions). Bo. S. S.
(4) 'Edition of the Gaüdovaho' (No. 1). Bo. S. S.
(5) 'Kumâragrâlacharita' (in the Press, No. 1.). Bo. S. S.
(6) 'The Atharvaveda with Sâyana's Com., discovered by Mr. Pandit, and published for the Government of Bombay (in the Press).
(7) 'Vedâsthayatra,' not completed, a serial translation of the R. V. into English and Hebrew.

II. K. T. Telang:—

(8) 'Edition of Bhartrihari's Centuries' (No. 1, two editions). Bo. S. S.
(9) 'Bhágavaddgîta' translated. Sacred Books of the East, vol. xviii.
(10) 'Was the Rámáyana copied from Homer?'

the minute thoroughness of the old indigenous school, can yet in favoured instances quit the old grooves and expatiate in the wider field opened to it by the vigour and enterprise of European learning. This tribute is due to the not inconsiderable group of young native scholars who, in the Bombay Presidency and the region subject to its influence, have maintained and still maintain the national honour in the beloved field of national learning, while they accept and employ in a truly catholic spirit all the resources placed at their disposal by the great brotherhood of erudition throughout the world.

III. R. G. Bhándárkar:—

(11) 'Edition of Mâlatîmâdhava' (one vol.). Bo. S. S.

(12) 'Report on the Search for S. MSS.' 1882–3 (vol. 1). Government Press.

(13) 'Report on the Search for S. MSS.' 1883–4 (vol. 1). Government Press.

(14) 'History of the Dekhan for the Bombay Gazetteer.'

(15) 'Wilson Lectures on Indian languages' (published in the Year). Bombay Branch, Royal Asiatic Society.

IV. Apte.

(16) English-Sanskrit Dictionary.

(17) Sanskrit-English Dictionary.

(18) Guide to Sanskrit Composition.

V.–VI. Parab and Godbole.

The Daśakumâracharita with the Comm. of Kavindra Sáiasvati and Sivarâm Tiwaro; and many other editions, with Commentaries for the Nirnayasâgra Press.

e.g., Sâkuntala, with the Arthadyotanikâ, Priyadarśikâ, by Srî Harsha, Kathâsaritsa Sâgara, etc., etc.

Yet if one without pretensions to be an expert may hazard the observation, the general out-turn of Sanskrit teaching, even in the Elphinstone and the Dekhan Colleges of the Bombay Presidency is stunted and meagre as compared with the needs of the community and of the age. The ordinary students just pass the examinations and obtain their degrees on a very slender minimum of true critical scholarship. A certain limited command of Sanskrit is most easily acquired by those whose vernacular language rests so largely on a Sanskrit foundation, and whose daily converse teems with Sanskrit phrases. But this kind of rote-knowledge need not necessarily imply a more thorough scholarship than a courier's acquaintance with French or Italian. The B.A. who takes up Sanskrit as his classical language does no doubt go a good deal further than that, but still not far enough for a vivifying formative influence to be exercised over him, still less for his powers to become in their turn productive and add materially to the sum of human knowledge and the volume of intellectual harmonies amongst mankind. I should even say, from observation, that Sanskrit, studied with anything like exclusiveness and made almost the sole ground of mental exertion during those years in which a permanent stamp is given to the intellectual and moral character, is apt in ordinary cases to exercise a narrowing and self-involving influence, to give acuteness and verbal skill, while hardening and confirming local and national conceit and disinclination to receive instruction from without. It would be invidious to cite particular evidences of this; but they must be manifest to anyone who closely observes the movements of native society at such a place as Poona. The position taken up by many Hindu scholars with reference to women and their place in human society shows that there may be genuine and extensive learning of a kind with but little moral expansion, and but slight enlargement of the capacity to appreciate the means by which India and the Hindus may contribute nobly to the future progress of the human race.

There seems, then, to be needed, even for the full appreciation of the Sanskrit literature and philosophy, much more than a technical mastery, however perfect, of the mere language itself. A liberal —that is, a wide-reaching—education is essential to the Sanskritist in India as in Europe, if he would make his learning fruitful and an element of human progress. It should be informed with philosophy, with the thoughts and emotions that have a universal and eternal value. This liberal education means for the Hindu (and indeed equally, or still more, for the Musalman) a thorough immersion in European thought—not in mathematical or physical science, which has its high and separate value, but in the thought which is concerned with the proper activities of men as individuals and as members of society. Fertility, expansion, even a true conception of what each system contains and can do for man, must be got at by bringing the European and the Asiatic systems into close contact and comparison. For this the Indian scholar should resort to the great fountain-heads of Western thought in the Greek literature, and follow the stream down through the philosophers and historians who have pourtrayed, and partly made, the living progressive world in its successive phases down to our own day.

The study of a literature or a philosophy—the one blends with the other—thus pursued is as far as possible from deserving a sneer or a reproach as impractical. The favourite notion of fifty years ago, that the world could be regenerated and human happiness secured by the mere *laissez-faire*, and the mechanical operation of barbaric self-acting laws of supply and demand, has been discredited by experience. Human society, human welfare and progress, it is now seen, present ever new problems, which demand for their solution a deeper insight into man's nature, a larger and more generous sympathy with his spiritual needs, than were dreamed of in a past generation. After a long fascination by the marvels of science, and the boons it has bestowed on our material existence, men's minds once more turn from the new standpoint thus gained towards a corresponding advance in their intellectual and moral being. The air is full of announcements of schemes for giving men more leisure, for making them more mutually helpful, for satisfying aspirations towards a beauty and completeness of life in which the soul may find rest. The time has once more arrived for the speculative and creative faculty to do some great things for the relief of man's estate. The more minds there are brought to bear on this work, and the better skilled and furnished they are with various endowments and experience, the greater will be the prospect of success. It appears to be the scheme of Providence, or a necessity of human nature, that many problems of society should first be wrought out on a limited scale, as amongst the Hebrews and the Greeks, before the results become available to mankind at large. Each nation stirred by great impulses may hope that it will have its own definite contribution to give towards the growth of our race in power, nobleness, and moral beauty. The Hindu and the Musalman have their contributions to make, but, in order to present these in shapes that shall be effectual and productive, they must gain a wide intellectual outlook. They must qualify themselves to see and to grasp those subtile links which bind human activities in a substantial unity amid endless phenomenal diversities. Thus trained and disciplined, they may, with their fine contemplative powers, become the interpreters of the special experience of their own people—of their specific message to mankind—in forms intelligible and acceptable to all nations. They will thus repay their debt to England and to Europe by a bounteous contribution to the sources of our future welfare, to an enlarged philosophy, a wider benevolence, and to "the mighty hopes that make us men."